Handmade book
Soft Form Relief Paste on textured kozo paper

Contents

*Sketchbook work
Printing and embossing*

Handmade books

*A knight and
his castle*

Introduction

The motivation for this book stems from an exciting archaeological dig very near to my home in North Yorkshire. Loftus lies between Whitby and Guisborough and it was here that a Saxon burial ground was discovered in 2007. In 2011 these artefacts were put on display in Kirkleatham Museum, near Redcar, and it was this exhibition that inspired me to write this book.

The jewellery from the Saxon Princess Exhibition is both intricate and exquisite and influences some of the textile pieces in this book. (Pages 57-59)

The Yorkshire moors is an area I know well and it can be both beautiful and harsh. It remains wild and untouched and it is therefore easy to imagine what it must have looked like in the 7th century AD. Loftus is surrounded by arable land on one side and moorland on the other. The landscape is scattered with memorial stones and the ruins of Whitby Abbey and Guisborough Priory are nearby.

A small part of this book focuses on the landscape that the Saxon Princess would have been familiar with and includes some poetic license.

The stylish young man opposite very kindly allowed his photograph to be taken at the Whitby Goth weekend. Inspiration from medieval times influenced his handmade accessories. He sports a red rose and obviously supports the House of Lancaster.

Medieval art and architecture has always held a fascination for me and was my starting point for an ongoing study that led me to many interesting places in Spain, France, Italy, Belgium and the UK. I have included some of my observations in this book.

Saxon to medieval times, leading up to the Renaissance spans many centuries and the items featured in this book are not intended to be a faithful historical representation of life in those times.

Using modern day fabrics, mixed media products and new techniques all of which are suitable for embroidery has been my focus.

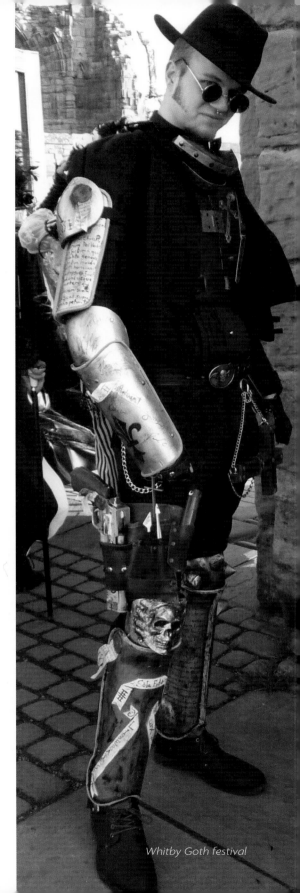

Whitby Goth festival

CHAPTER ONE

Embroidering With Paper And Fabric

I really like creating fabrics from scratch and I eagerly explore any way in which to do this.

The projects covered on the next few pages are all inspired by the landscape that the Saxon Princess would have been familiar with. The Yorkshire moors, where she is from, can be both beautiful and harsh.

It can be sunny on the moorland but it is often beset by grey skies and the moors are sometimes shrouded in mist. This can be oppressive and at other times, when combined with frost it can shimmer and have an ethereal quality.

Ridgeways were formed on the moors in medieval times as travellers pulled carts over the rough uneven ground. These ridgeways are still evident today.

The fabric for the handmade book represents the ridgeways on the moors. It is made from cocoon strippings. These are coloured with coffee and embellished with sheer fabrics and nappy liners, burnt back using a heat tool. Black webbing spray gives added dimension.

Ridgeways on the moors

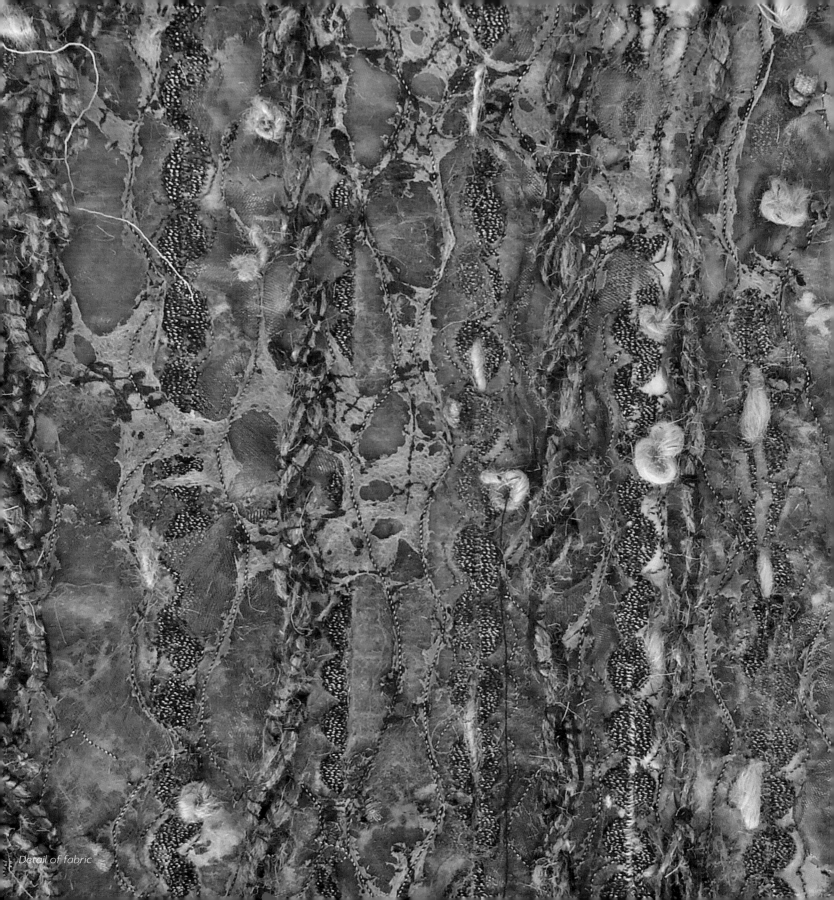

Detail of fabric

Crochet Or Knitting Using Thin Papers

The needle case illustrated opposite was also inspired by the ridgeways on the moors.

The choice of paper is crucial for this technique. The fabric used to make book covers or needle cases must be robust but it must also be tactile. Strips of newspaper are too brittle and do not feel tactile and long strips of bookbinders tissue, teabag paper or thin papers made from lokta or kozo papers are preferable.

This technique involves sandwiched layers.

- The bottom layer should be an open weave fabric. I used Hessian for this. If you use a closely woven fabric for the bottom layer you will not be able to embroider using a thick yarn.
- The second layer will be crocheted or knitted paper.
- The third layer will be thick and perhaps some thin yarns.
- Beads are optional

Work like this:

1. Cut long strips of thin paper about 2cms wide. I used long strips of teabag paper. You could use a paper shredder for this technique.

2. Knit or crochet using the paper strips. You are looking for textures so do not worry about making a perfect fabric. Just persevere with the breakages. Make joins on the back. I crocheted my paper as illustrated below.

3. Paint the crocheted fabric. More than one colour usually looks best. Use thin water based paints. I used Brusho and highlighted occasional areas with gold paint. Acrylic paints will alter the feel of the fabric and will not be as tactile.

4. Spray 505 repositionable glue over the back of the paper fabric.

5. Bond it to the open weave fabric of your choice. I used Hessian.

6. Use thick yarns and twisted thread stitch to embroider over and between the crocheted paper and into the Hessian.

7. Add beads if desired.

Partially painted crocheted paper

Ridgeways on the North Yorkshire moors

Crocheted Paper For Vessels

Thin paper strips can be used to crochet caps. These caps can then be made into a firm structure such as a vessel. To crochet with paper requires a little patience as the thin paper strips keep snapping. When joining papers do not worry about untidy ends. They will not be noticeable when the work has been completed.

I used this technique to represent the legend of the raven from Guisborough Priory.

Guisborough is on the edge of the Yorkshire moors and the ancient ruins of an Augustinian Priory dominate it. It was built in 1119 by the De Brus family and destroyed by fire in 1289. It was rebuilt in the Gothic style. In 1540 it was stripped in the Dissolution of the Monasteries. The east window still stands tall and erect and imposing.
(See page 72)

The legend says that there is a box of treasure buried in the grounds of the priory and that the treasure is guarded by a raven.

The misty moors, a raven's nest and the brilliance of gold, contained in the treasure, inspired the vessel illustrated opposite.

It is made from crocheted paper with cocos fibres added. Cocos fibres can usually be bought from garden centres. They are made from the husk of coconuts and are often bleached or coloured. I bought mine in a natural colour.

CMC powder is also known as carboxymethyl cellulose tylose powder. It is non-toxic and is used in the catering industry. It can be bought from cake icing suppliers and also from art suppliers. Mixed with water it makes versatile glue.

You will need:

- A vessel to use as a mould & plastic bag to cover it
- CMC paste
- Thin papers
- Crochet hook
- Water based paints such as Brusho
- Cocos fibres
- Gold paint
- Threads and needle

How I worked:

1. Cut the paper into long strips.

2. Use the paper strips to crochet a hat shape.

3. Cover a suitable vessel with a thin plastic bag. Tuck the ends of the plastic bag into the well.

4. Place the paper crocheted hat shape over the plastic covered vessel.

5. Paint CMC paste over the crocheted paper. Leave it to dry. (You could use diluted PVA)

6. Paint the paper whilst it is on the mould. I used Brusho.

7. Remove the vessel by pulling the plastic bag off the mould.

8. Add stitching in selected areas.

9. Cover the mould with the plastic bag again and then the stitched vessel.

10. Cover with cocos fibres. Seal these in position using the CMC paste.

11. Colour the cocos fibres and selected areas on the vessel. I painted mine gold.

Detail of "Cornfield" fabric

Embroidering With Paper Strips

Cornfields were an important part of life in Saxon and Medieval times and played a part in art. The two fabrics illustrated on the previous pages were made into bags. To make the fabric for my bags inspired by cornfields this is how I worked:

1. I began by stretching Hessian in a frame. (For an uneven surface this is not really necessary but you may prefer to work with it framed.)

2. 1cm wide strips of teabag paper were cut to use as a substitute for thread. You can use any thin paper but for wearable art it works best if the paper is tactile and flexible.

3. The fabric was embroidered in tent stitch. No attempt was made to keep the stitch regular but the stitches were sewn in a diagonal direction. (Fig 1) Do not bother knotting the end or trying to cast off. When the paper breaks just leave it exposed on the back. Bring all ends through to the back and do not leave any loose ends on the front.

4. Use paints of your choice to colour the paper. (Fig 2) I used Brusho as I wanted it to remain tactile. Water based paints are preferable as they are more tactile than acrylic paints.

5. Because my fabric was going to be used for wearable art I backed it with cotton batting prior to stretching it in a frame again. A stabiliser of some sorts is needed because the Hessian is so open. I used 505 spray glue to bond the Hessian to the batting.

6. Use threads or ribbons of your choice to embroider over the painted paper stitches. You may need to use a leather-sewing needle to execute this.

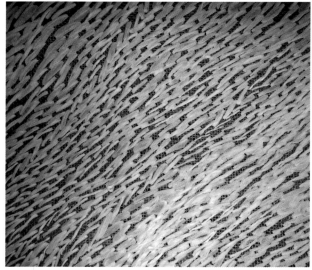

Fig 1

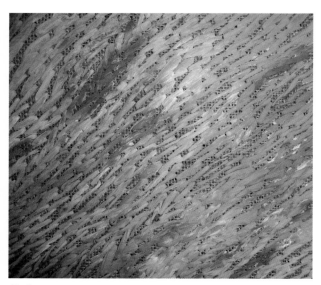

Fig 2

Shosenshi Viscose

I wanted to create a fabric that was tactile and was made up of multiple stitches. In the previous pages I worked on top of thin papers. You can substitute other materials such as those made from Lutradur for the bottom layer. Sarah Wise used Lutradur strips for her example illustrated below. I decided to work with Shosenshi viscose. Shosenshi viscose is flat paper yarn made from 100% linen. It has a viscose sizing and the yarn feels crisp. It is sold as a specialist knitting or weaving yarn but it is great for embroidery too. You could use raffia as a substitute. Raffia will create fabric with a harder texture.

Stitching using this linen tape is easier than stitching with paper because it has strength and it does not keep snapping. It does make a firm bed to work on and the crispness of the paper leaves it feeling a little crunchy. Further stitching using a soft thread eliminates the crunchy feel. Jan Pilgrim worked with it in her sample below.

Shosenshi viscose fibres-linen tape

Samples of stitching on top of stitches made by students in Australia can be seen below.

Marion Webb

Jan Pilgrim

Nola Helmore

Sarah Wise

Lapis Lazuli Needlecase

1. I worked on a loose open weave linen fabric and covered it all with Sorbello stitch using the Shosenshi paper yarn. An open weave is desirable to enable the multiple layers of threads of varying thickness to pass through.

2. I painted selected areas with Brusho.

3. Then layers of stitches were worked on top using the same stitch but thick threads.

4. Beads were sewn in selected areas and lapis lazuli stone beads were also included.

Needle case

Plotting Against Richard III

This is a panel for a bag. It represents Henry and Jasper plotting against Richard III before the Battle of Bosworth Field.

It is worked with blue shosenshi viscose. The soft tactile fabric is achieved by working with cotton thread on top of the Shosenshi viscose.

Henry and Jasper are appliquéd to the background fabric. They are made on white sheeting. Texture was added by stencilling light molding paste to the sheeting. Coloured scrim (gauze) was bonded to the sheeting by painting CMC paste over the layers of scrim and the sheeting. The Shosenshi viscose stitches were coloured with Brusho after the stitching had been completed.

Plotting against Richard III

Cushion with Celtic motif
Background-Canvas work stitches using thin papers and then thick silk threads.

Stone crosses

Machine Embroidered Paper Strips

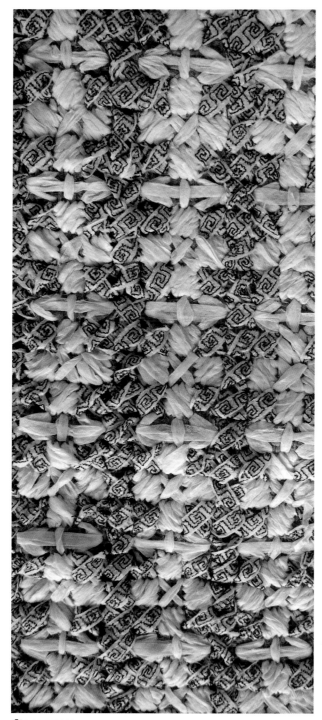

The landscape on the Yorkshire moors is scattered with stone crosses and markers. Many of these memorial stones have legends attached to them, dating back as far as Saxon times. Some have been erected centuries afterwards. Not all are in the shape of a cross.

The photograph album illustrated on page 20 and the fabric illustrated opposite and page 22 form part of my study on stone crosses. They both involve the use of thin, machine embroidered paper strips.

For my first experiments I worked with stitch and tear. This paper proved to be quite stiff when used for hand sewing but it was easy to stitch the automatic patterns onto this type of paper. I created a needle case using this paper but then as stitching with it was unwieldy to hand stitch I then moved onto working with thinner, more fragile papers. I found these more suitable for pieces that are tactile.

Stone crosses
Stitch and tear

Machine embroidered strips

Reverse Applique - Cut Back Work

I worked with thin paper on Hessian fabric in order to achieve the sculptural effect needed for this photograph album. African bark cloth from the fig tree represents the brown earth. An open weave fabric such as Hessian is essential for the success of this technique.

As thistles are also part of the moorlands I decided to embroider in selected places using thistle top yarn.

This is how I worked:

1. Use an automatic pattern on a sewing machine to embroider long strips on thin paper.

2. Cut out the embroidered narrow strips.

3. Thread a bodkin with one of the strips.

4. Embroider using the strip.

5. Use thick thread to embroider in the spaces. I used thistle top yarn. My yarn had been spun by Rachel Powell -two thirds thistle tops and one third Soya (see pages 39, 40)

6. Place the work over a second fabric. I used fig bark cloth from Africa. Stitch into the layers.

7. Cut back selected areas.

8. Use thick yarn to sew again. I used thick silk thread to outline the areas that had been cut back.

9. Add beads if desired.

The completed photograph album can be seen on page 20. Further work using this technique can be seen on page 106.

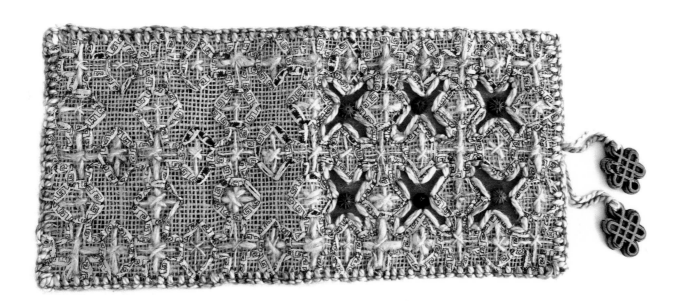

Fabric for stone crosses photograph album

Spinning, Weaving And Slashing

In this section the artwork represents spinning and weaving in medieval times. Fabric was torn into strips and used as yarn to embroider over an open weave ground. You could use sari strips for this technique. I cut my strips and coloured them with Brusho. (Sample below) This sample is now ready for further stitching on top of the sari silk strip stitching. It helps if the open weave fabric is backed onto a stabiliser for the last stages of stitching. I use cotton batting.

For the fabric illustrated on the opposite page I used scrim (gauze) with gold calligraphy printed in areas. The scrim is cut into strips and the lettering becomes illegible. The scrim frays but that is an essential part of the finished piece.

The aim was to cover the whole of the background fabric with stitches. Potato sacks were used for the background fabric because the fabric has an open weave and will take the wide strips of fabric with ease.

1. I used a sewing machine to embroider lines in long strips using an automatic repeat pattern. I used white thread. You could use coloured thread and personalise your fabric strips using an automatic pattern from your sewing machine. I wanted mine to be subtle as the resulting fabric was for a wedding album.

2. These embroidered strips were then cut out.

3. The strips were threaded in a needle and used to embroider Twisted chain stitch on a potato sack.

4. The potato sack was bonded to cotton batting with 505 spray glue.

5. Silk sacks on silk yarn were couched in selected areas and pearl beads added.

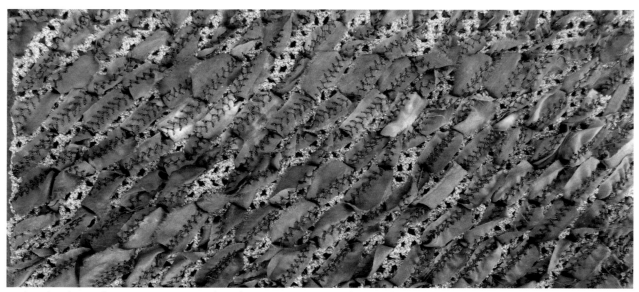

Embroidered sari silk strips sewn over crocheted netting representing chain mail.

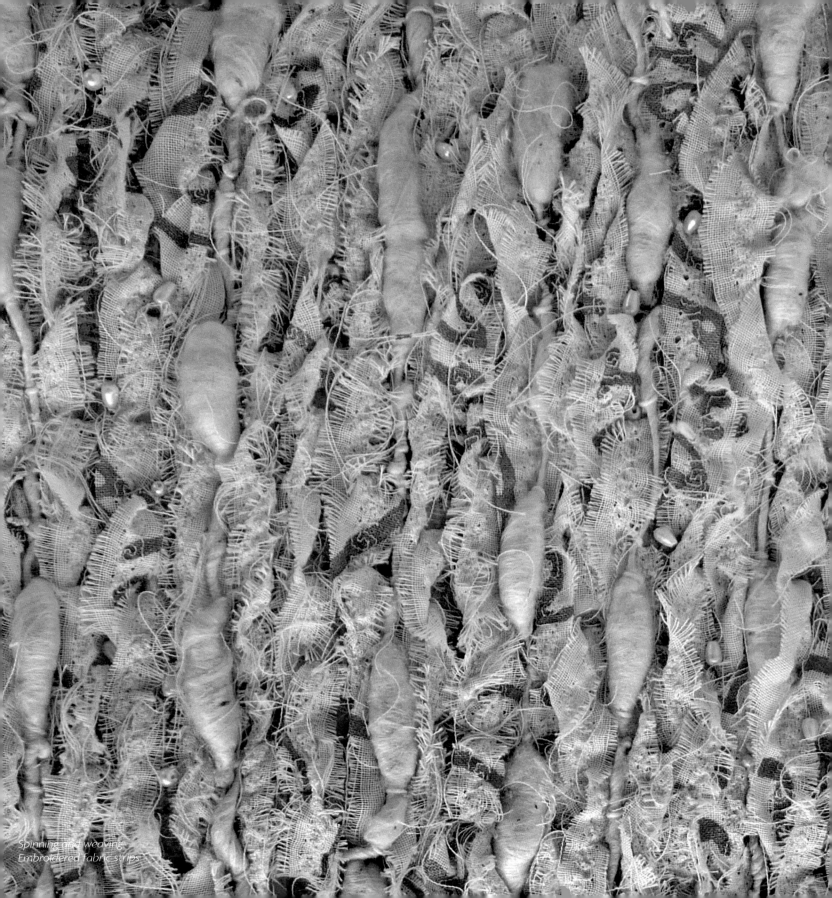

Spinning and weaving
Embroidered fabric strips

Chain Mail, Spinning And Weaving

It looks as if it is a long way from my inspiration but the fabric illustrated opposite was inspired by the fabrics on the dresses worn by ladies in paintings by Filippino Lippi, Ghirlandaio and Benozzo Gozzoli. The white or ivory coloured luxurious fabrics embroidered in gold and made from silk made a big impression on me. Chain mail worn by knights came into the equation and the notion of chain mail, spinning and weaving was born. This is how I worked:

1. I began by making the background fabric. The background fabric is handmade silk paper, coloured lapis lazuli blue.

2. Gold thread was used to sew automatic patterns in straight lines on cream coloured silk fabric. Fig 1

3. These long strips were cut out.

4. Silver crochet thread was used to crochet the chain mail. Fig 2

5. The long strips of embroidered silk were woven through the crocheted chain mail. Fig 3

6. Silk sacks were embroidered using gold machine embroidery thread, using detached buttonhole stitch. Fig 4

7. The silk sacks were appliquéd in position. The resulting fabric is illustrated on page 26.

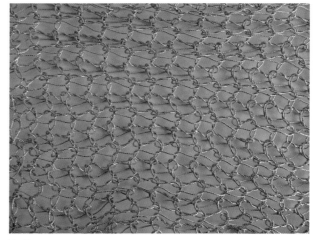

Fig 2

Fig 3

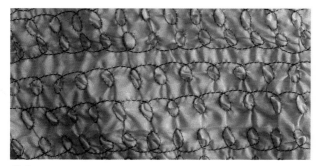

Fig 1

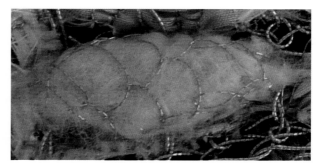

Fig 4

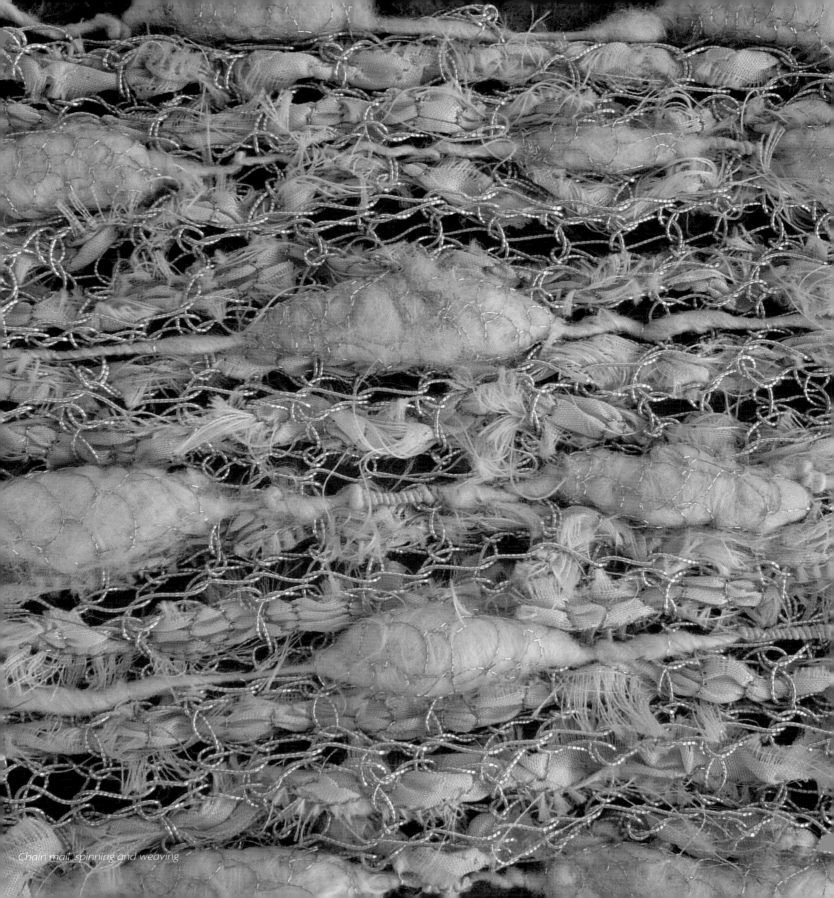

Chain mail, spinning and weaving

Cocoon Strippings. Honesty Petals & Kozo Bark

It is no secret that I like to work with silk fibres and silk cocoon strippings. The fabric on the opposite page was inspired by the Ca d'Oro Palace, Venice. It is built up in layers.

- Silk scrim
- Encaustic wax
- Silk flats or rods
- Cocoon strippings
- Snippets of thread
- Embroidery thread
- Bondaweb
- Honesty petals
- Silk noil thread
- Kozo bark
- Fuse FX or Misty Fuse

This is how I worked:

1. I wanted a luxurious fabric with natural colouring. I used silk scrim for the bottom fabric. To make it represent the water lapping round the building it was partially coloured with dark green encaustic wax. The wax was ironed on sparingly so that it did not dominate.

2. Dark green silk flats (ironed silk rods) were cut up, distorted and placed in selected areas.

3. Cocoon strippings were pulled so that they were thin, open and lacy. These were laid on top of the silk scrim.

4. Silk and cotton snippets of thread in a natural colour were placed in selected areas. They were placed so that they overlapped and in places were trapped under the cocoon strippings.

5. Water was sprayed over the sandwiched layers.

6. The damp layers were covered with non-stick baking parchment. A hot iron was used over the parchment to fuse the strippings to the silk scrim.

7. Cream coloured linen thread was used to embroider Backstitch and Running stitch in selected areas.

8. The fabric was covered with Bondaweb fusible webbing and this was ironed to fuse the webbing to the fabric. (Non-stick baking parchment was used over the layers to protect the iron.)

9. The papers were removed and honesty petals were placed in selected areas.

10. The fabric was covered with parchment again and it was ironed to fuse the petals.

11. Hand stitching using silk noil thread was used in selected areas.

12. Bleached kozo bark was cut to shape and bonded and appliquéd to the fabric.

13. The fabric was covered with white fusible webbing. I used Fuse FX but you could use Misty fuse. Cover the layers with baking parchment before ironing.

14. I repeated this last action so that the webbing became more obvious.

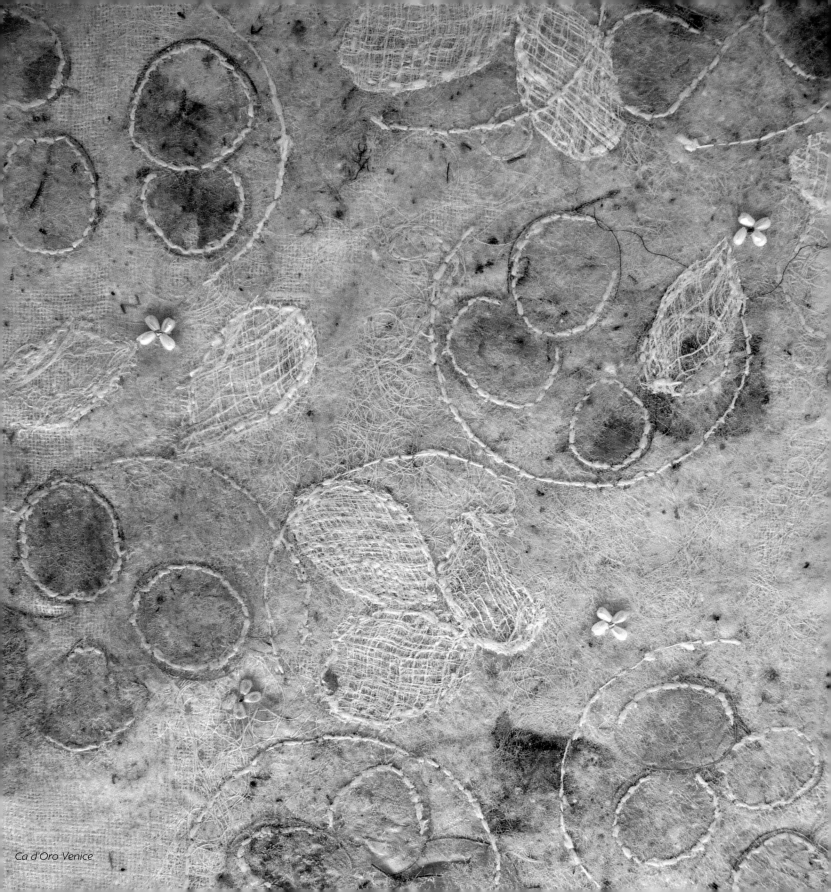

Ca d'Oro Venice

CHAPTER TWO

Stained Glass

Gothic buildings with their towering columns, stained glass windows and richly painted walls have always impressed and inspired me. The rose window in York Minster fascinated me as a child. In medieval times the rose windows were known as wheel windows and it was only in the 17th century that we came to call them rose windows.

War of the Roses and the rose window, to celebrate the union between the Royal Houses of York and Lancaster in York Minster, the paper roses presented to diners on the Pride of Bruges ferry by Brian Lirazan along with the rose window in Chartres Cathedral all contributed to the inspiration for my artwork.

1. The rose window opposite is made on textured kozo paper.

2. It is coloured with blue encaustic wax. Brusho paint is added by blending the colours using a wet baby wipe.

3. The paper is sealed with acrylic wax.

5. The motif in the centre is made from impressed glue.

6. The petals of the rose window are trapped between two sheets of Bondaweb.

7. Angelina fibres are ironed and cut to shape and the bonded petals applied.

8. The kozo paper is backed onto cotton batting using 505 spray glue.

Paper rose
Brian Lirazan

Petals trapped between two sheets of Bondaweb

Rose window

Soft Flow Clear Medium

Colourcraft Soft Flow Clear Medium can be made into an acrylic skin. It can be coloured in the early stages of the process and then it can be used for appliqué to represent stained glass windows. I worked with it in a variety of ways. This is how I made the fabric to appliqué the shapes illustrated on the book on the opposite page:

1. Cover the edges of a sheet of glass with masking tape.

2. Pour a generous amount of the Soft Flow Medium onto the glass.

3. Use a clean paintbrush to spread the medium over the glass.

4. Sprinkle a very small amount of Brusho powder over the medium on the glass. You will find that you do not get pleasing results if you are heavy handed with the Brusho. It is an amazingly small amount that is required.

5. Leave it to dry. As it dries the Brusho spreads and colours run into each other. Do not be tempted to touch the medium until it is completely dry.

6. When it is dry you can peel it off the glass.

7. You can use this for appliqué on fabrics of your choice. (Below, right and page 32. A further example can also be seen on page 68)

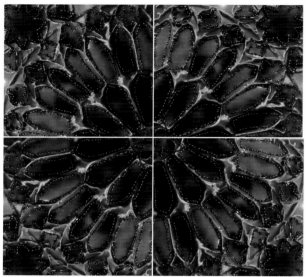

Soft Flow skin appliquéd to Soft Form Relief paste

York Minster- Rose window
Soft Flow Clear medium, Brusho and Soft Form Relief Paste

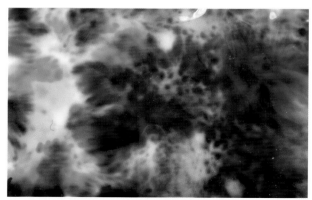

Brusho powder on a Soft Flow Clear skin

31

Handmade book
Stained glass windows on painted kozo bark

Inkjet Printing On Soft Flow Clear Medium

I wanted to know if I could inkjet print onto a skin made with Soft Flow Clear Medium. This time I spread the medium onto the sheet of glass and left it to dry. When it was dry I peeled it off the sheet of glass. I had made it thick enough to go through my printer without a carrier sheet. All I needed to do was cut it to A4 size. After printing it should be left for an hour and then the inks should be stable. Back it onto a light coloured stabiliser prior to stitching.

It is fun to experiment with Soft Flow Clear Medium. I tried mixing it with Golden clear granular gel. The granular gel inhibited the spread of the Brusho and the extent of the colouring is reduced, leaving more plain spaces. I inkjet printed a black and white image onto this skin.

Inkjet printing on Soft Flow Clear medium
Image © CSG CIC Glasgow Museums

Inkjet Printing On PVA

For the experiment below I tried mixing regular PVA with washing up liquid. It became very runny and I had to add more PVA to thicken it. It was still rather runny but I went ahead and allowed it to drip and run off the sheet of glass. I always work on non-stick baking parchment so that any overflows are contained on that. Brusho was sprinkled over it.

When it was dry I was pleased with the results but found that it was very thin and flimsy and acted rather like cling film. To inkjet print on it I used a carrier sheet with masking tape. When it had been printed I backed it onto white Funtex (page 43) so that stitching became easy and the PVA fabric was stable. Although this technique worked I found the Soft Flow Medium easier to work with.

Inkjet printing on a PVA skin

Stone buildings and stained glass
Image © CSG CIC Glasgow Museums

Newspaper vessel based on stone walls

Stone Walls & Stained Glass

My newspaper bowl represents stone walls, with stained glass windows set in them.

Inside the bowl there is an image from a medieval stained glass window.

The image was inkjet printed onto Lazertran. This was ironed off onto thin white paper. (See page 85) The covering for the inkjet printed image was made like this:

1. Soft Flow Clear medium was poured into small containers.

2. A tiny amount of Brusho powder was added to each container, using different colours. The mixture was stirred in each container using a clean brush.

3. The mixture was poured out of the containers onto a sheet of glass.

4. A paintbrush was used to spread the colours so that they were next to each other but not overlapping. Some bleeding will occur.

5. When it is dry it can be peeled off and used for appliqué.

The stone walls were made from rolled and twisted newspaper strips.

1. You can make your own long strips of twisted newspapers or you can buy it as paper string. Begin by cutting long strips of newspaper that are roughly 2cms or 1 inch wide.

2. The paper strips are made by rolling long lengths and twisting them and joining the next length on so that you have a continuous length. You might find it quicker to use a spindle to twist the newspapers but I found that it was possible to do it by hand.

3. These newspaper strips can be laced together to form a flat coil. To do this take care not to lace the strip on top of the previous row. Ensure that the strips are side by side.

4. When the circle is big enough you can build the sides up to the required height. To build the sides up you do this by lacing the next layer of paper strip on top of the previous layer as opposed to lacing them side-by-side.

5. (Image on page 36)

Texture For Fabric & Papers

CHAPTER THREE

Textured paper
Embossed book cover

Pulp Papers

In this chapter I had great fun working with a variety of papers and fabrics. It was a joy to collaborate with some of my colleagues whilst exhibiting at the Glasgow Sewing for Pleasure Show. Jonathan Korejko is a talented pulp papermaker. He loves to pass on his skills to young and old alike. You can see him in the image below working on his fabulous stand at the Glasgow Sewing for Pleasure and Hobbycraft show.

Jonathan makes a vast variety of interesting pulp papers and it was great fun to use his thistle tops and to work with his papers.

Rachel Powell was also at this show and she too collaborated with us as illustrated on the opposite page.

Rachel Powell on her stand

Jonathan Korejko on his stand at the Glasgow show

Thistle Tops

Jonathan collected thistle tops and made his version of thistle top pulp papers with them. The resulting paper is thin, smooth and appears to have tiny hairs trapped in it. This appealing paper is very porous and soaks up any mixed media. You can work with it in a variety of ways.

When you inkjet print in black and white or stamp using a black inkpad onto thistle top paper the hairs shine through in a most attractive way. The end result looks a little like marble and I felt it was a great way in which to represent the marble images depicted on the front of the Cathedral in Lucca. (Image on page 42)

With the thistle tops that Jonathan gave to me I made cocoon stripping paper with thistle tops trapped in it. I found it necessary to trap the fine thistle tops in a layer of Bondaweb, fusible webbing. I scorched the cocoon stripping paper with the hot iron to make it stronger and also to make it more in line with the colour of the thistle tops.

Rachel Powell was also given thistle tops to work with and she had great fun spinning thistle tops, even though they did fly all over her stand!

The thistle top yarn is two-thirds thistle top and one-third Soya. I have used it to embroider on the Stone Crosses photograph album on page 20.

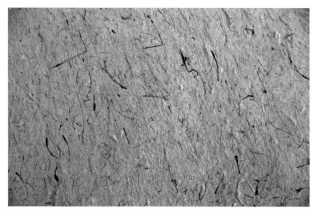

Thistle top pulp paper

Thistle top pulp paper with thistle tops trapped in it

Thistle tops

Thistle tops spun into yarn

St. George and the dragon
Drawing copied by Xantha Hall when she was studying John Ruskin.
Thistle top paper

Façade –Duomo Lucca
Thistle top paper

Die Cut Machines And Funtex

It seems appropriate to add a word about die cut machines before I proceed with this section on embossing. These tools are used by card makers and scrap bookmakers. They are dual purpose in that the mangle type mechanism can be used as an embossing tool and also as a die cutter to cut out images. There are lots of different makes available such as Sissex, Big Shot and Cuttlebug. They are sometimes just referred to as die cut machines.

Embossing folders are made for card makers to use with card or paper. You open the folder, insert your paper, put it through the die cut machine and the paper takes on the embossed pattern. The limitations are the size.

You can emboss pelmet Vilene, silk papers, cocoon stripping papers, waxed teabag paper, H250 interfacing and a multitude of other smooth fabrics such as calico, sheeting or copper foil. I used it to emboss Funtex as illustrated below. Funtex is made by Freudenberg, the company that makes Vilene. It comes in many colours and it is rather like felt but thinner. I used it a lot as a stabiliser and also to inkjet print on it. To inkjet print on it cut it to A4 size and print directly on it. It is firm enough to go through the printer. I used it to inkjet print the images on pages 3, 76 and 77. The images were cut out and embossed using the die cut machine.

The Funtex scroll illustrated below, left, was made by covering Funtex with coloured paper. Automatic patterns were embroidered in straight lines using a sewing machine. Back the Funtex onto Bondaweb prior to cutting the shape out. This enables you to bond it to another fabric more easily. When the scroll is cut out it is textured because of the intensive stitching. It remains thin enough to appliqué and does not stand too proud on the fabric it is appliquéd to.

Funtex scroll cut out using the die cut machine

Embossed Funtex

Book cover inspired by the De Brus- cenotaph in Guisborough church
Image of knight on thistle top paper
Background —embossed silk paper

Rub Ons And Embossing Plates

This technique is quick and easy as it takes very little drying time and this can be a bonus on one-day workshops!

I used thistle top pulp paper, made by Jonathan Korejko and rub on waxes such as Treasure Gold or Gleam. Any bought fairly smooth pulp paper or handmade paper will work for this technique.

How I worked:

1. I used the Big Shot machine and an embossing plate to emboss thistle top pulp paper. The paper was put through the machine twice to increase the width-hence the fold in the paper. This is where the spine will lie. Fig 1

2. Metallic rub on Gleam paste was rubbed over the embossed shapes. Fig 2

3. Gold wax was rubbed over the top. Fig 3. (I used Goldfinger.)

4. To seal the colours I painted Shimmer Mod Podge over the paper. Shimmer Mod Podge dries leaving a golden shimmer over the paper.

5. I used Tim Holtz alcohol inks and then the blending solution to add the final layer of colour. Fig 4

6. The paper needs to be put on a stabiliser prior to stitching. I ironed the pulp paper to the shiny side of H250. Remember to cover the artwork with baking parchment when you iron.

Fig 2

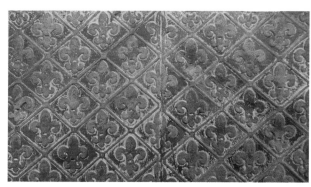
Fig 3

Fig 1

Fig 4

Embossed thistle top paper,
Spine made from embossed copper shim.

Embossing Piles Of Thin Papers

If you layer up a pile of thin papers such as teabag paper, thin kozo papers, or even thin toilet papers you can, without much effort, make them into robust papers for stitch. These papers can be sandwiched together and an embossed pattern can be made by putting them through a die cut machine. When you stitch into this pile of thin papers you will achieve a quilted effect without having to use batting or a stabiliser.

For a book cover you will need:

- Thin papers
- Embossing folder
- Die cut machine

Method:

1. Cut 5 pieces of thin paper to size. You could use teabag paper, thin kozo paper, toilet paper, tissue paper or bookbinders repair tissue. To cut my paper to fit into the embossing folder I cut it slightly wider than the width of the embossing folder and slightly longer than double the length of the folder.

2. Place the pile of papers in the embossing folder.

3. Run them through the machine. You need to exert as much pressure as possible in order to sandwich and emboss all of the layers so that they are held together.

4. Put the other end of the papers in the embossing machine and emboss these. You will have a join where they have been placed next to each other in the embossing folder. This will be the spine and will not be seen.

Nappy liner and pile of embossed papers

Thin Papers And Nappy Liners

Nappy liners are not so easy to find these days but large stores still sell them. They are beautiful to work with because they are semi-transparent and tactile. Try layering one over a pile of papers and emboss it on the die cut machine. The nappy liner will take on the embossed pattern but it will not be as obvious as the patterned embossed papers.

The use of a nappy liner will make the pile of papers more tactile and robust.

If you decide to colour the paper you can colour the pile of papers before or after embossing them. You could use sheer coloured fabric as the top layer instead of the white nappy liner.

Spine

For the spine I used silk paper. The pattern was painted using gold bronzing powder mixed with acrylic wax. (Remember the safety precautions when working with powders.) Gold or bronze relief paste made by Colourcraft will also work well when used as paint.

Embroider the fabric for the spine and then appliqué it so that it covers the embossing join.

Embossed papers and nappy liner

CHAPTER FOUR

Casting Images

Cast paper on vegetarian silk background

Cast paper coloured with Relief paste and alcohol inks
Motif made using gold Soft Form Relief paste and colour added with alcohol inks

Solusheet Casting

Solusheet knight formed over a plastic incised plate

Solusheet cross

Solusheet can be used for all sorts of things. Apart from machine embroidered lace it can make interesting casts. Solusheet is a water-soluble fabric.

I wanted my casts to be strong, robust and to be able to take colour and hand stitching. I worked like this:

1. Work on a surface that has an incised pattern. You could use incised metal or plastic, a carved wooden block or a rubber stamp.

   Note that sometimes , especially on carved wooden stamps you may need to use a thin layer of Vaseline to act as a barrier. This enables you to remove the dry cast more easily. The carved block and the Solusheet cast can be cleaned afterwards using a baby wipe.

2. Cut 3 pieces of Solusheet slightly larger than the pattern you want to transfer.

3. Cut another piece of thin paper to this size. I used teabag paper but you could use toilet paper or thin kozo paper.

4. Place the layers of Solusheet on top of your stamp. Have the thin paper facing you as the last layer.

5. Use your finger to sparingly apply water to the layers. The image will begin to appear. Continue until the whole of the image is visible. Ensure that you go to the edges. I like to go beyond the edges so that the thin paper becomes stuck to the Solusheet layers. This can be trimmed off afterwards. Leave it to dry. When it is dry peel it off the mould.

6. You can now paint your cast. The resulting casts are semi transparent. Use thick paints to colour them as opposed to watery paints. I used silver rub on Goldfinger wax to colour the knight and the crosses for the Saxon box. Colourcraft Soft Form Relief paste also works well. (Page 61)

Reliquary box
Solusheet patches on silk paper-
Silk paper textured in the Big shot using an embossing folder.

Casting Paper

The cheapest way to create a cast that can be stitched into is to make a paper cast.

Selecting a suitable mould is the key to this project. To begin with try working on rubber stamps or carved wooden blocks.

The resulting casts can be painted and appliquéd to fabric or can be stand-alone motifs.

They can be stitched into prior to appliqué. This is often desirable, as needle marks in the wrong area will show.

You will need:

- Plasticine
- Thin paper
- Incised pattern to make a mould
- Diluted PVA
- Paintbrush
- Vaseline- optional depending on the mould

Paper cast
Impression taken from a carved wooden block

Making the cast paper:

1. Work Plasticine in your hands until it is malleable.

2. Press it into a mould. The mould should have texture. The deeper the incised patterns are the better the cast will be. If necessary you could rub a thin smear of Vaseline over the mould prior to pushing the Plasticine over it.

3. You might find it easier at this stage if you place the mould with the Plasticine in a fridge or a freezer to harden. I don't usually bother.

4. Gently peel the Plasticine off the mould. It should have incised patterns transferred to it.

5. Vaseline from the mould may be transferred to the Plasticine. Use your finger to rub this over the mould. Use a baby wipe to remove traces of Vaseline from the mould.

6. Thin papers applied in layers work best. If you use thick papers your cast may resemble cardboard. You could use any thin papers. Some toilet papers work well. Tear the paper into pieces.

7. Use a paintbrush and diluted PVA glue to cover the Plasticine mould with paper layers. As an alternative to PVA glue you could use CMC paste. For thin more fragile pieces use 3 layers of paper only.

8. Leave to dry.

Paper cast bonded to textured handmade paper

Reliquary box
Light molding paste

Reliquary box
Light molding paste

56

Lid for scallop shell box

Scallop shell evening purse
Light molding paste

Scallop Shells

The scallop shell is featured a lot in medieval times. It pops up all over the place. People aspired to make pilgrimages to holy shrines and Santiago De Compostela was a popular destination. The lines on the scallop shell represent the notion that all roads led to the shrine. People often wore badges depicting a shell to show that they had visited a shrine.

Over the past few years I have visited a lot of places housing medieval art. In the Ducal Palace at Urbino the shell was used for decoration all the way round one of the rooms.

The shell is featured on the De Brus cenotaph from Guisborough Priory, now in Guisborough church. It also is evident on the jewellery worn by the Saxon princess and now displayed In Kirkleatham museum in Yorkshire.

I decided I wanted to make a paste evening bag and also a lid for a scallop shell box. These are illustrated on pages 57 and 58.

This is how I worked:

1. I used the largest scallop shell I could find.

2. A Plasticine cast was made from it.

3. Light molding paste by Golden was spread over it and left to dry.

Painted paste

4. Red, yellow and blue acrylic paints were used in designated areas.

5. When it was dry Shimmer Mod Podge was painted over the whole of the paste.

6. Tim Holtz alcohol inks were used to add the final layer of colour.

7. The paste was stitched into and beaded.

Collection of scallop shells

Silk paper book
Motif made from Colourcraft soft Form Relief paste

Colourcraft Soft Form Relief Paste

This is a new thick paste medium made by Colourcraft. It has many applications and it comes in a variety of colours. It can be used to stencil or it can be used as paint.

The Solusheet knight was painted using gold and bronze Relief paste. To make the Solusheet knight see page 51.

The doorway was made using the clear paste. It was painted with the bronze paste, stitched into and then sanded back.

Gold paste was used to stencil the castle. The castle is on cocoon stripping paper. The paper was painted with acrylic paints. Then it was re-painted with Relief paste.

Relief paste doorway

Solusheet knight

Castle stencilled in gold relief paste

Texture can be added to surfaces if you brush a heavy layer of the paste onto your fabric. You can then push lace into it or a stamp. You will not get a faithful impression but you will get an interesting textured surface.

This relief paste can be made into a stand alone paste fabric and it feels like rubbery gel fabric and it is not as porous as other pastes such as Golden light molding paste. It is possible to gain an impression using a very thin layer of paste.

You cannot stamp successfully into paste medium but you can obtain a motif that is suitable for applique if you spread the paste over a rubber texture mat and leave it to dry. I have made similar motifs in this way using Golden light molding paste explained in my book co-written with Maggie Grey.

The technique works well over rubber texture mats as these are pliable and the paste fabric can easily be removed. You will know when the paste is dry because the pattern will show through onto the back.

If you want to make motifs using wooden carved blocks then the technique is somewhat different. The carved block is not pliable and the paste will be extremely difficult to remove.

The way round this is to first make Plasticine casts. Sometimes the addition of Vaseline can be an advantage. The technique for working with Plasticine casts is explained on the following pages.

Wooden carved stamps

Working With Plasticine

To make my Saxon box this is how I worked:

1. Push Plasticine into the carved wooden block and then remove it. Decide whether to use Vaseline or not. Vaseline is only necessary if you do not want the colour of the Plasticine to transfer to the relief paste fabric.

2. Use a spatula to spread a thin layer of Colourcraft paste medium over the Plasticine mould. The paste comes in a variety of colours.

3. Leave it to dry. It will take a long while to dry out thoroughly, especially if you use Vaseline. I leave mine in a warm place for one week.

4. To remove it from the Plasticine. I find it easier to ease the edges before attempting to peel it off as a whole.

5. Trim the edges if necessary.

6. Use a baby wipe to remove any traces of Vaseline. If you did not use Vaseline then traces of the Plasticine will remain. Use a sharp point to dig out the Plasticine, being careful not to puncture the paste motif. Some colour from the Plasticine will remain. If you paint a sealer such as Shimmer Mod Podge over the cast then the colour will be sealed in as illustrated below and opposite.

Base for Saxon box

Tall Saxon box with removable lid

Embossed Soft Form Paste Medium

Colourcraft Soft Form Relief Paste medium can be made into a stand alone fabric and then it can be embossed. To make the paste fabric work like this:

1. Use a spatula to spread a generous layer of paste onto a silicone craft sheet or Teflon baking sheet. Do not use non-stick baking parchment because as the paste dries on such parchment it begins to ripple. You want a flat piece of paste fabric for these techniques. Spend some time smoothing the paste out to achieve a level layer. I used copper paste to make the "fabric" for the dome of the box illustrated on the opposite page.

2. Leave the craft sheet in a warm place to encourage the drying process. I left mine under a hot radiator for 24 hours.

3. When the paste is completely dry it can be removed from the craft sheet. The resulting "fabric" will be smooth on the side that was placed next to the sheet. This paste fabric is different to others in that it has the feel and appearance of gel. It can be made so that is very thin.

4. To emboss the paste fabric place it in a plastic embossing folder and run it through a die cut machine. Too much pressure will act like a cutting tool. If it is only cut in one or two small areas then it is still suitable for use.

5. Add colour if desired. My copper paste fabric was very shiny and looked too new so I knocked the colour back with Tim Holtz alcohol inks.

6. You can stitch into the paste fabric without a stabiliser or you could bond it to forming felt as I did.

Shaping Reliquary Boxes

To shape the boxes illustrated throughout this book I have worked with Softsculpt heat mouldable foam or forming felt.

Forming felt is great to work with because you can stitch into it easily. Examples of Saxon boxes made using forming felt can be seen on pages 52, 70, 90.

Forming felt is so called because if you position it as desired and lightly spray it with water it then holds its shape when dry.

Working with forming felt is my preferred method for shaping the lid for boxes. Sometimes it is advantageous to use forming felt for the structure of the box and then line the shaped box and base using thin Softsculpt. If the edges of your box are not rigid you could cut wooden kebab sticks, wrap them with yarn and appliqué these to the edges. See page 52.

Softsculpt heat mouldable foam can be used for the outside of boxes. I like to impress the foam and cover it with a thin layer of silk paper. If there are any tears or gaps in the silk paper then this is brilliant because it ages the fabric and represents decay. Softsculpt treated in this way is suitable for both the outside and the inside of these boxes.

When used inside it resembles worn leather. An example can be seen on page 97.

Saxon box
Embossed paste dome
Silk paper base

66

Making Your Own Plates For Embossing

The brass of Margaret Peyton has inspired a lot of my artwork. The image is illustrated on page 77. Initially I made a printing block and used the fabric on Margaret Peyton's dress as inspiration. I printed onto fabric using blue paint.

Later I decided to use the same soft carve printing block with relief paste. The inspiration for this artwork was the intarsia woodwork seen in the Ducal Palace at Urbino.

This is how I worked:

1. To make the printing block I first drew my design on paper.

2. The design was traced onto the printing block.

3. Lino cutting tools were used to carve out the shapes. Fig 1

Fig 2

Fig 1

4. Soft Form Relief paste was spread over the carved printing block using a spatula to do so.

5. The paste was left to dry overnight in a warm place.

6. You will know when it is dry because the pattern on the block will show through. Fig 2

7. Carefully go round all of the edges to loosen the paste. Peel it off the block. As you pull, it will stretch and distort, but it will bounce back into position.

8. The side that was next to the block will have raised ridges. These raised ridges are great for containing mixed media or for appliqué. I tried using Soft Flow Clear medium fabric coloured with Brusho for appliqué. (See page 31)

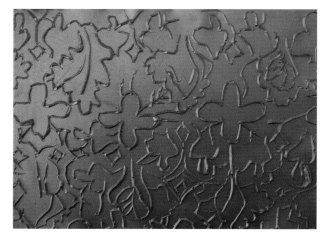

Fig 3

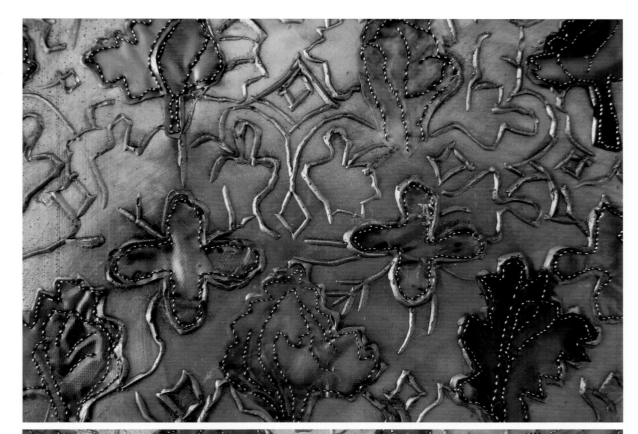

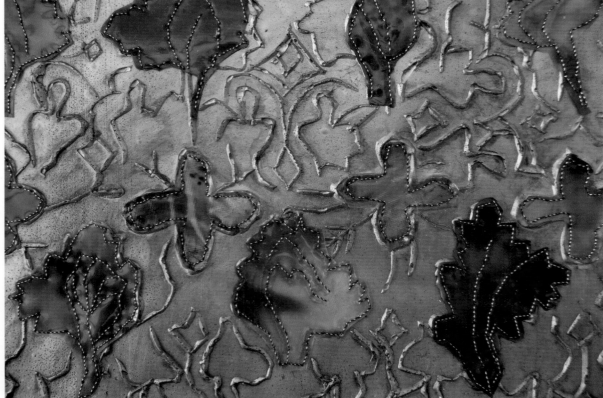

*Soft Flow Clear medium fabric with
Soft Form Relief paste fabric formed
over a soft carved printing block*

Marbled Soft Form Relief Paste And Soft Flow Clear Medium

Relief paste mixed with Soft Flow Clear medium makes a unique fabric for stitch.

I used the resulting fabric to make a Saxon inspired reliquary box with a difference. My box is a musical box.

This is how I made the fabric:

1. I began by pouring the Soft Flow Clear medium into a container.

2. Then coloured Soft Form Relief paste was added. I used gold.

3. The sticky mediums were poured onto a sheet of glass and spread using a paintbrush. Brusho paint was sparingly sprinkled over the pastes.

4. I waited a few minutes and then used my finger to draw into the pastes. Do not over mix the colours.

5. Leave the pastes to dry.

6. When it is completely dry it can be peeled off the sheet of glass. At this stage care should be taken so that it does not fold back on itself. When it has "cured" a little longer this should not be a problem.

7. Add colour using Tim Holtz alcohol inks if required.

8. I used forming felt for the structure for my musical box.

Marbled relief paste and Washable PVA

Musical box
Marbled relief paste and PVA

Inkjet Printing Gold Soft Form Relief Paste Fabric

Guisborough Priory was founded in 1119 but it now lies in ruins. Guisborough church is situated next to the ruins and inside the church there is a large cenotaph made from granite. Robert de Brus arrived in England from Normandy and was granted estates in this area by William the Conqueror. The cenotaph memorial was made in 1520 and commemorates knights from the De Brus family. De Brus knights from the English and Scottish sides of the family are depicted on the cenotaph box.

My box, illustrated here is based on the De Brus cenotaph. The base fabric for the box is made from silk paper. The images were inkjet printed onto gold relief paste fabric. They were stitched into prior to being appliquéd to the silk paper.

The box shape is made from cardboard and was bought from a craft shop.

De Brus box
Scottish and English knights depicted round the sides

De Brus box
East window of Guisborough Priory on the lid

Inkjet Printing And Embossing The Paste Medium

A large sheet of relief paste medium will look rather flat and boring and it will look like a sheet of plastic. To give it added interest try texturing it and then inkjet printing or stamping.

Work like this:

1. Make a sheet of relief paste fabric as explained on the previous page. If your craft sheet has not been cleaned from a previous project there will be traces of paint or paste on it. If you leave these traces in place and spread the relief paste over it then these traces may become incorporated in your relief paste fabric. This is how I achieved the distressed appearance seen in the illustration opposite.

2. When it is dry remove it from the silicone craft sheet.

3. Position this over a carrier sheet. A carrier sheet could be an A4 sheet of computer paper.

4. Trim the edges of the paste fabric so that they do not protrude.

5. Bind all 4 edges of the sandwiched layers using masking tape.

6. Inkjet print onto the embossed paste fabric. Remember not to infringe copyright laws. My image is taken from a stained glass window in The Burrell collection in Glasgow and is copyrighted © CSG CIC Glasgow Museums

7. Leave the image to dry for 24 hours and then remove the masking tape and the carrier sheet.

8. Place the printed fabric between a plastic embossing folder and emboss it in the die cut machine.

9. Use 505 spray glue on the back of the fabric to bond it to a stabiliser. A stabiliser could be H250 interfacing, pelmet Vilene, Funtex or cotton batting. The choice of stabiliser is dependent upon the use for the fabric.

10. Hand embroider the fabric. I intended this image to be used for the cover on a handmade book. The background fabric is textured kozo paper. As it is heavily textured it would have been difficult to stitch into the relief paste with some accuracy. The beading and outline stitching was completed first and then the whole was appliquéd to the coloured textured paper. The book cover can be seen on page 2.

Gold relief paste fabric, embossed and inkjet printed
© CSG CIC Glasgow Museums

CHAPTER FIVE

Innovative Ways For Printing

Amiens Cathedral

Many fabrics can be used for inkjet printing. Sometimes it is necessary to apply a medium so that the inks are stable. Golden Digital Ground or InkAid are brilliant for this job. They are in liquid form and you paint it over the fabric, allow it to dry and then you can inkjet print on it. If you paint it over a porous fabric then the medium will seep through to the other side.

Work on baking parchment and do not be tempted to lift the fabric until it is completely dry. The fabric for the book cover illustrated opposite and below is garden weed suppressant. Garden weed suppressant is porous and Golden Digital Ground was used to prepare the surface prior to inkjet printing. Cut the weed suppressant to A4 size. Back it onto a carrier sheet of computer paper. You cannot bond it to freezer paper because the weed suppressant buckles with heat. Use 505 to temporarily bond the weed suppressant to the carrier sheet and bind the edges with masking tape.

If you allow the Digital Ground fluid to seep through to the back of the fabric it will collect in puddles on the baking parchment. You can use this to your advantage. When the fabric is dry turn it over and the back can become the front. If you stamp or inkjet print on this side you will obtain some interesting results.

Weed suppressant
The back becomes the front

Funtex And H250 Interfacing

H250 interfacing is made by Freudenberg. It has a shiny side and this is where the glue is. To activate the glue you position the interfacing shiny side down onto the fabric of your choice and iron. To inkjet print you do not iron it onto any fabric. You inkjet print onto the plain side and not the shiny side. You can inkjet print on Funtex and H250 without using Digital Ground. You will get a paler image. To hand embroider the inkjet printed fabric you do not need a stabiliser. To machine embroider then you may wish to use a stabiliser on the H250 interfacing.

1. Cut the fabric to A4 size.

2. Print onto the fabric.

3. Cut out the image.

4. Place it in an embossing folder and run it through a die cut machine to emboss it. (Page 3 and page 77)

H250 interfacing on textured silk paper

Habotai Silk And Lazertran

How I worked:

1. The white areas are made by drawing using a tjanting tool and batik wax.

2. The areas in between are coloured with silk paints.

3. The wax is ironed out of the fabric.

4. An image is inkjet printed onto Lazertan.

5. The Lazertran is ironed onto the silk fabric.

6. The backing paper is removed from the Lazertran.

7. The back becomes the front so that the plastic side is no longer visible.

8. Stitching takes place when it is placed over cotton quilters' batting.

Silk and Lazertran image

Margaret Peyton-Medieval Brass
Inkjet printed onto H250 interfacing
Silk paper background

"Innocence"
See page 86

Bark Cloth And Kozo Bark

This chapter deals with a variety of techniques for transferring images by hand or machine.

It was after a visit to the ducal Palace in Urbino that I became fascinated by medieval wooden ornamentation. There are fabulous examples there of intarsia, the Italian craft of wooden inlay. It reminded me of the work done in a much lesser scale in Sorrento, where we lived for a number of years. I then became more interested in wooden choir stalls that I had seen in various places and in particular the wooden sculptured friezes in Amiens Cathedral. Once I was set on this line of thinking I attempted to make my representation in fabric.

The idea of making textiles resemble wood but still be able to stitch into it was my inspiration. I initially decided to work with kozo bark. There are varying grades of kozo bark, made from the mulberry tree. There are also varying prices depending on how much work has been done to it. African bark cloth is made from the bark from fig trees and is brown in colour.

I decided to experiment using as many different types that I could find.

I began by working with closely intertwined fibres in bark cloth. Normally when I am working with kozo bark I wet it and pull the fibres to create more distortion. This time I only wanted to work with kozo bark that had the fibres more closely woven together.

Image drawn on kozo bark
Inspired by the front of the Cathedral in Lucca

Inkjet Printing On Kozo Bark

If you inkjet print or stamp onto bark cloth part of the design will be lost because the cloth is so open. To overcome this problem work like this:

1. Select an area that is closely knit and discard areas that are very open. Cut the cloth to size.

2. Place the cloth on the shiny side of H250 interfacing. Cover with baking parchment.

3. Iron to bond the layers.

4. Depending on your printer you can inkjet print onto the fabric. My printer preferred me to back the layers onto computer paper as a carrier sheet. To do this I sprayed the back of the H250 with 505 repositionable glue. I used masking tape to enclose the edges. Whether you are using a carrier sheet or not it is advisable to enclose the edges with masking tape.

Stamping On Kozo Bark

1. You may want to paint or stamp an image onto your bark cloth. Prepare your cloth in the same way as if you were inkjet printing. (i.e use a backing fabric underneath.) I found that H250 was a good fabric to use for these techniques.

2. Do not use an inked stamp to print as the image will not be satisfactory. Use acrylic paint or thick heat fixable paints on your stamp to obtain good results.

USING DIGITAL GROUND

If you want a really vibrant image printed on the bark you could consider preparing the kozo bark as described above. When it is bonded onto the H250 paint it with Golden Digital Ground or Inkaid. Allow this medium to dry prior to inkjet printing or stamping.

Inkjet printed and painted kozo bark
Inspired by the Cathedral in Lucca

Charcoal Pencils On Bark Cloth

The design on the bark cloth illustrated opposite was inspired by patterns carved on the clothes of the medieval wooden carved figures depicted on a frieze in Amiens Cathedral. My bark cloth was closely woven but I still ironed it onto H250 interfacing prior to commencing any artwork.

I worked like this-

1. I used a rubber stamp to stamp a design. The pattern did not matter because I knew that the ripples on the cloth would prevent an even printing. The colours did matter because these were to be the background colours. I used a 5 colour rainbow Big and Juicy inkpad. On the previous page I cautioned about stamping using an inkpad on bark cloth because the fabric is uneven and the whole of the pattern will not be transferred. In this instance it did not matter.

2. After studying the design on the dress of one of the wooden models on the frieze in Amiens Cathedral numerous sketches were made.

3. The chosen sketch was traced onto tracing paper.

4. The tracing paper image was transferred to the bark cloth. My bark cloth was light in colour so this made things easy.

5. Derwent fine art charcoal pencils added the colour to the traced design.

6. Acrylic wax was painted over the bark cloth to set the charcoal.

7. Linen threads in greys and blues were used to outline the shapes.

8. Tim Holtz alcohol inks were added for depth of colour.

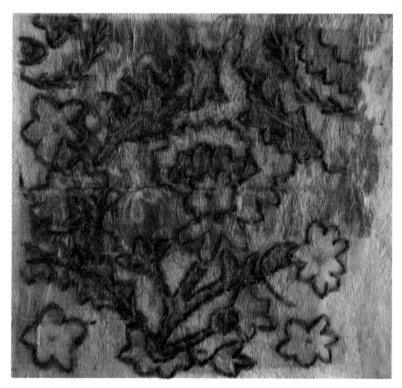

Bark cloth with charcoal drawing

Lid for an intarsia effect box.
Bark cloth with charcoal drawing.

Stamped Tapa Or Bark Cloth

This design is inspired by a pattern on the dress of Margaret Peyton depicted in a medieval brass in 1484. (Page 77)

To create a stamp based on this design I used copper foil and a heat mouldable foam block. I used the printing block on tapa cloth or bark cloth.

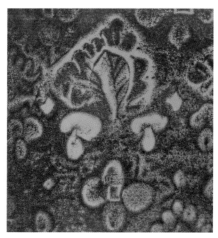

Stamp tried on white card –not to scale

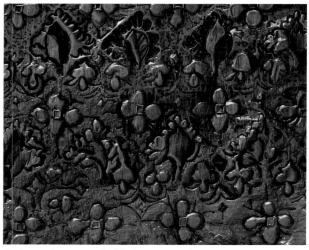

Embossed copper relief foil-not to scale

Work like this:

1. Draw your design on tracing paper.

2. Transfer the design to copper foil. I use A4 size copper relief foil sold for children. It is copper coated foil and is cheaper than the real thing but does the job. To transfer the design place an old magazine on the work surface. Position the foil on top and finally the drawing. Use masking tape to temporarily bind the 3 layers together.

3. Use metal embossing tools to trace over the design and thus transfer the pattern.

4. Remove the tracing paper. Use the embossing tools to gain more relief. (Illustrated above)

5. Use a heat tool to heat a foam-stamping block.

6. Immediately press this into the embossed copper shim.

7. Back the fabric onto a stabiliser. I wanted a padded effect so I used cotton batting. To bond the layers together I used 505 spray glue.

8. Use an inkpad or thick paint to cover the surface of the new stamp. Press onto the bark cloth and repeat the pattern as illustrated below.

Stamp and inkpad used on bark cloth

9. Stitch into the fabric.

10. Seal the fabric with a sealer of your choice. I used gloss Mod Podge. This deepens the colour.

Bark cloth vessel representing intarsia work

Lazertran On Paper

There are many ways in which images can be transferred to fabric. It is so quick and easy nowadays. The downside can be that the image may end up with a plasticised finish and this is not always desirable. The images on the following pages were obtained using a variety of methods. Remember you may need to flip the image if you want it to be in a certain direction.

To use Lazertran inkjet transfer paper all you have to do is select your image and size. Print it onto the inkjet paper. Wait a day and then transfer the image onto fabric by ironing. The instructions are on the packet.

It can become quite interesting if instead of transferring the image to fabric you transfer it to paper instead. The choice of paper is important. The thin papers I worked with are bookbinders tissue, teabag paper or thin lokta paper.

The image transferred onto the paper plant pot was ironed onto thin paper, cut out and stitched into. It was then glued to the paper on the vessel using CMC paste.

The images on the next four pages were inspired by a fresco in Pickering church in North Yorkshire.

Paper plant pot with Lazertran image

Lazertran-The Back Becomes The Front

This time I wanted to transfer the image onto paper, leaving the plasticised printed image on the back.

I used:

- Lazertran transfer paper for light clothes
- White thin paper
- Iron
- Baking parchment
- Kozo bark
- H250 interfacing

This is how I worked:

1. Cut the kozo bark to size.

2. Bond it by ironing it to the shiny side of H250 interfacing.

3. Select the image and size it.

4. Inkjet print the image onto Lazertran inkjet paper for light clothes.

5. Cut the image to size.

6. Remove the backing paper.

7. Place the inkjet printed image on thin paper with the bright side facing you.

8. Cover with baking parchment and iron to transfer the printed image.

9. Cut the thin paper to fit the printed image.

10. Turn the image over. This now becomes the front.

11. Use 505 spray glue to bond the image to the kozo bark.

12. Stitch into the image. Outline the image so that it is secure.

I called this image "Innocence". It depicts part of the story of Samson and Delilah. She is not at all innocent but she looks demure. She is carrying a plate and her hands are shaped like forks. (Detail can be seen on page 78.)

Innocence

Lazertran On Its Own

The Pickering fresco bowl illustrated opposite is very large and measures 38cms in diameter.

To work on these images the backing paper was removed and I worked on the plastic skin. I found it easier to work like this:

1. Inkjet print the image onto the Lazertran.

2. Remove the Lazertran paper backing.

3. Stitch into the floppy plastic. As I wanted it to remain thin I did not back it onto a stabiliser.

4. When the stitching was complete I bonded it to the vessel using CMC paste. I was able to bond the stitched images on the inside and outside of the vessel.

5. To make the vessel have the appearance of a flaking fresco I used Paper Artsy acrylic paints and Paper Artsy crackle glaze.

6. The rim was decorated with machine embroidered paper. To do this I used an automatic pattern to stitch onto white thin paper. The paper was bonded to the rim using CMC paste.

7. To knock back the images I used black fusible webbing. You could use Fuse FX or Misty Fuse for this.

Lazertran skin

Pickering fresco

Embossed Softsculpt And Image Transfer

Embossed Softsculpt

Image taken from a photograph.
© CSG CIC Glasgow Museums

In the past I have used heat and then pressure to transfer raised detail to Softsculpt and thus emboss it. Sometimes I find it difficult to exert the pressure required to push a wooden carved block or something with raised detail into the heated Softsculpt to achieve this result.

Recently I have found it very satisfying to place Softsculpt in an embossing folder and then run it through a die cutting machine as explained on page43.

Note that too much pressure can puncture the Softsculpt.

I used foam, embossed in an embossing folder and put through the Big Shot machine to cover the box illustrated on this page and on pages 91, 92.

On close inspection I discovered that I had in fact bought different types of heat mouldable foam. Some of the A4 sheets were denser than others. The foam illustrated on the left hand side is smoother than the foam illustrated on pages 91, 92. This makes a difference when applying rub on waxes.

The Burrell box
Images from stained glass in The Burrell collection.
© CSG CIC Glasgow Museums Collection

Colouring The Foam

Image printed on Lazertran

I like to work with gold bronzing powder mixed with acrylic wax. This makes fabulous paint but you should remember the safety precautions when working with bronzing powders.

As an alternative I sometimes use a rub on wax. For me the problem with rub on waxes is that they rub on but also rub off. If it is to be used on something that will be handled a lot then this can sometimes be overcome by sealing the rub on wax. The sealer could be acrylic wax or one of the Mod Podge mediums. These both alter the appearance.

To colour the Softsculpt I used Goldfinger rub on wax. It is more expensive than most but it does stay in place. And it does not make a mess. It does not need a sealer to protect it.

The images were made by inkjet printing onto Lazertran and then ironing it off onto thin paper. The image was bonded to the embossed Softsculpt by 505 spray glue.

I was delighted that the Glasgow Museum department allowed me to use images that I had photographed from the stained glass in The Burrell collection and my thanks go to them.

The Burrell box
Images from stained glass in The Burrell collection.
© CSG CIC Glasgow Museums Collection

Millefleurs poppy field
Painted baby wipe

Inkjet Printing On A Baby Wipe

I love the Millefleurs tapestry, "The Legend of Saint Eloi, in Beaune and it has inspired me to work on a number of artworks over the years. The tapestry is filled with flowers and bushes and the Saint is leading a romantic white horse. The horse tramples on the flowers and nothing is to scale. I have worked with this theme in various ways and the image illustrated opposite is the starting point for one of them. I used a photograph to inkjet print the image onto a painted baby wipe.

I like to paint using wet baby wipes instead of a paintbrush. This works really well if you are painting a background and want colours to merge and blend. When you have finished painting keep the coloured baby wipe for another project. This technique works with any paint but you should wear gloves to protect your hands.

The field of flowers illustrated opposite was worked on a coloured baby wipe. Millefleurs tapestries have dark coloured backgrounds with some depth of colour so if you are trying to represent this then the colours on the baby wipe should be dark.

Work like this:

1. Use a coloured baby wipe. Any type of paint will do to colour it but it looks best if the colours are not too muddied.

2. When it is dry straighten it without stretching it and distorting it.

3. Spray 505 repositionable spray glue on the back.

4. Bond it to a sheet of computer paper and use this as a carrier sheet. Use masking tape to cover all of the edges round the baby wipe. This will prevent it from coming loose.

5. Inkjet print your image onto the baby wipe.

6. Remove the masking tape and the carrier sheet.

7. Back the baby wipe onto a stabiliser. I like to use cotton quilter's batting for this. I use 505 glue to bond the layers. Cut the stabiliser larger than the baby wipe so that it can be stretched in a frame for hand stitching.

8. Add mixed media as well as embroidery if desired. I used Liquid Appliqué in selected areas. This product is made by Marvy and is coloured puff paint for use on fabric or paper.

9. You can now embroider the baby wipe.

Printing Using Blocks And Cutting Tools

Cutting into lino blocks is not for everyone because you need strong hands and control. Sadly I do not have this. Happily we can now buy soft carve blocks and these are much easier to use. Some are A4 in size and this means you can carve blocks of A4 size ready for repeat pattern printing.

The book cover illustrated opposite was printed with one such block. The design was improvised from clothing depicted in Gentile Da Fabriano's Adoration of the Magi. This painting, held in the Uffizi, is full of pattern and a simplified version of one of the patterns was used here. The paper was marbled using oil paints prior to being printed.

I wanted a simple design and so I drew directly onto the block using a biro. I then used lino-cutting tools to carve into the block.

You could trace your design onto the block. Use a pencil to draw your design on to tracing paper. Reverse the paper and go over the design again. Then place it on the block and go over the lines a third time to transfer the design onto the block.

To print on the paper illustrated below I first coloured the paper by marbling with oil paints.

When the paper was dry I used the carved block to print my design. I used acrylic paint to print on the marbled paper. See page 67 for other uses for the block.

Marbled and printed paper

Paper marbled with oil paints and then printed using a soft carve print block

Rustic box
Softsculpt covered with silk paper.
Architectural detail-embossed cocoon stripping paper

Celtic bag
Bubble wrap, textured kozo paper

CHAPTER SIX

Other Mixed Media

PATTERNED FOIL

Gentile Da Fabriano's Adoration of the Magi in the Uffizi art gallery was the inspiration for this fabric.

It is made from cocoon stripping paper.

This is how I worked:

1. I made a substantial piece of cocoon stripping paper, layering up the strippings and bonding them with the heat from the iron and water sprayed liberally over them. (Do not forget the non stick baking parchment)

2. Both sides of the cocoon stripping paper were sealed with acrylic wax.

3. The paper was cut to size.

4. The bag was painted using diluted coffee.

5. Brown shoe polish was sparingly added using the shoe brush. This added a little surface detail.

6. The fabric was painted using gloss Mod Podge. This leaves a plasticised appearance but it also makes it robust and waterproof.

7. When this was dry it was covered with patterned gold foil. Place the gold foil with the matt side down.

8. Cover this with baking parchment and iron.

9. When it is cool peel off the foil.

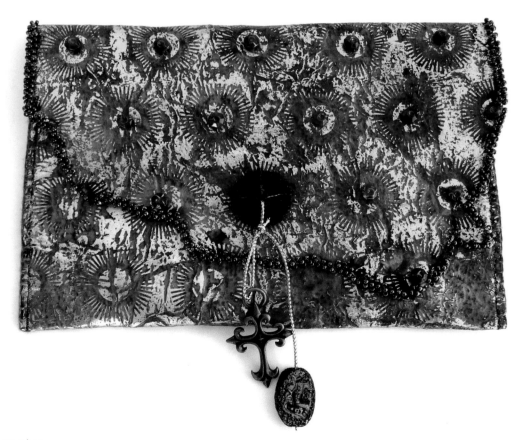

Cocoon stripping bag

Hand made book
Foiled Crash fabric

Fusible Thread

Charlotte's Fusible thread is used mainly for appliqué. This thread is made by Superior and it should be used with Superior Monopoly invisible thread in the bobbin. Nylon invisible thread is unsuitable because of the heat you will be applying at a later stage.

Fusible thread and foiling techniques are fun to work with. Use a sewing machine to sew using this thread and then foil can be bonded to the stitches.

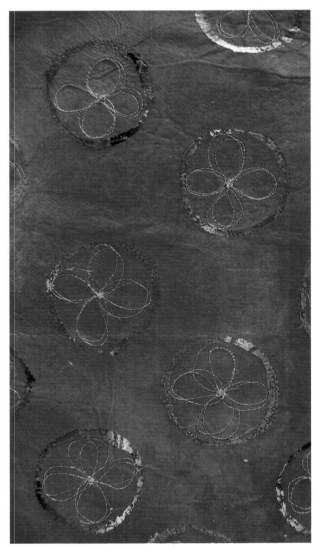

Silk paper fabric
Foil on fusible thread

Work like this:

1. Select a top stitch needle for use in the sewing machine.

2. Use Monopoly invisible thread in the bobbin.

3. The fusible thread needs to be on the top spool because the stitches need to lie on the front of the fabric.

4. Select the fabric of your choice. I used silk paper because it is smooth.

5. Stitch into the fabric. A single line of stitching does not show up well so it is better to go over the same area a few times if you are using a straight stitch. Alternatively you can select an automatic pattern or zigzag pattern. The most important thing is to ensure that you are not pulling the Monopoly thread up, as this will prevent maximum foiling.

6. Place your fabric on baking parchment on an ironing board.

7. Position the foil coloured side up

8. Cover with baking parchment and iron to fuse the foil to the fusible thread. Wait until the fabric is cold before removing the foil. The foil will bond to the fusible thread.

The bag illustrated opposite is made from silk paper. The silk paper has been coloured and then waxed with acrylic wax and beeswax polish. Fusible thread was sewn in selected areas. When foil was placed on top and ironed it fused to the fusible thread but it also transferred sparingly to the waxed surface.

Harvest
Silk paper, burnished and foiled

Plasterer's Cotton Scrim

The turbulent years of warfare that led up to the War of the Roses and the relationship with France inspired me to create a body of work based on this uncertain time.

I wanted the fabric to appear to be fragile but in fact be robust. I used open, lacy fabrics to convey this.

Plasterer's cotton scrim can be bought from specialist suppliers or builder's merchants. It can be bought on long rolls and is about 3 inches wide and is impregnated with glue. If you use this in conjunction with a thin solution of CMC paste you can build up layers that will produce thin, fragile looking but sturdy vessels. If buying from a builder's merchant you need to ensure that it is made from cotton and not sticky backed plastic.

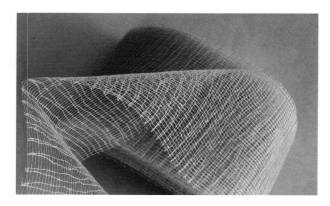

My Fragile vessel illustrated opposite was made from plasters scrim, silk skeleton leaves, laminated teabag paper and cricula silk. Cricula silk is hard to the touch but can be used for couching and embroidery. (Page 105)

I worked like this:

1. Place a plastic bag over the vessel of your choice. Tuck the ends into the well of the vessel. The plastic is there to protect the vessel.

2. Cut the scrim into rectangles about 3 inches wide. (8cms).

3. Mix a thin solution of CMC powder with water to make a paste. The solution needs to be thin. If it is thick it will dry and be noticeable.

4. Use a paintbrush to apply about three layers of the scrim strips to the mould. Begin at the base and work up from there.

5. Leave it to dry. When it is dry pull the plastic out of the well and ease it off the mould. Remove the plastic and check for any large holes.

6. Place the plastic back over the vessel and return the vessel to the mould. Cover any places that need another layer of scrim.

7. Paint the vessel with thin water based paints.

8. Place the skeleton leaves in position and glue these in place.

9. When it is dry you can laminate the centre with thin coloured paper if desired. To laminate it place the paper in position and paint over it with the CMC paste.

10. When it is dry it can be removed from the vessel and the plastic bag removed from the centre.

11. I used cricula silk for the rim. The silk is yellow in colour.

Fragile –Uncertain times

Cricula Silk Pods

Cricula silk pods come from Indonesia. The pods are hard, but they are open and lacy and golden in colour. They are easy to stitch into because they are so open.

To work with them I ironed them flat and in some cases tore them apart. These pods have already been spliced open. (Fig 1)

The pods are easy to trap in cocoon strippings. Wet the pods as well as the cocoon strippings. Iron with a hot iron. I like to scorch the fabric so that it looks caramelised. Fig 3

The silk itself is firm to the touch. I found it ideal to use round the rim of my vessels. (Fig 2 and page 104)

It is a little unwieldy to stitch with but in conjunction with other yarns it can be satisfying to work with. I worked with it on top of coloured embroidered strips of paper that had been used to embroider over an open weave cotton fabric. (Illustration on the opposite page and technique on page 21.)

Fig 1

Fig 2

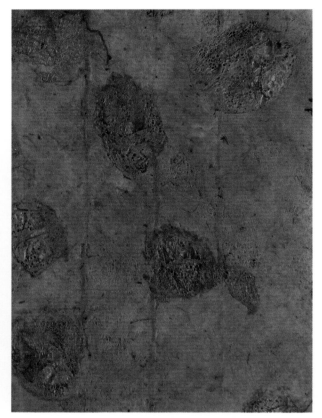

Fig 3

Cricula silk over embroidered paper

Hunting dog – seen in The Burrell Collection
Funtex and H250 interfacing

Miniature boxes and handmade books
Colourcraft Soft Form Relief Paste – larger box coloured with silver Goldfinger wax

Medieval inspirations
By ALISON WRAY-McCANN
Intricate works of art
fabbeads@talktalk.net

Medieval book
By JOSIE STOREY
Medieval book and pages made from Funtex

The hare leaves to explore
By KATH DANSWAN
Inspired by the Book of Illuminated Manuscripts and hunting scenes
Kath.danswan@tiscali co.uk

JHREN MIR A WELE
A LAN YR AFON
R NEILL HANHER
ED IDAW YN
LLOSGI OR&WREIDD
NYTY VLAEN

The tree of Mabinogion
By GLESNI WILLIAMS
Inspired by stories of Mabinogion. Peredur came to a valley where a tree was in fire.
Half was engulfed with flames and half was still wooded.
glesniheulog@aol.com

St David's Kilpeck
By WENDY DOLAN
The piece is inspired by the
magnificent door at the medieval
Church of St David in Kilpeck,
Herefordshire. The text is taken
from an old Anglo Saxon chronicle.
wendy.dolan@ntlworld.com

Celtic dragon photograph album
 By XANTHA HALL
The album is inspired by fiery dragons from legends of King Arthur.
xanthahall@hotmail.com

Stained glass windows
By PATRICIA FORSHAW
3d sections inspired by stained glass windows.
pmforshaw@btinternet.com

Peacock
By ALICE GOVE

*Knot Saxon paper
By JONATHAN KOREJKO
Pulp paper with linen,
hemp and cotton scrim,
thistle down and rabbit
fur. Surface decoration
includes blue leather,
horsehair, green linen,
hand dyed wood pulp.
www.timberland.co.uk*

Bringing the news
By CHRISTINE OSMAN
Wallpaper and mixed media

Medieval tiled floor
By ALISON McINNES
Hand dyed fabrics
alisonmcinnes73@hotmail.com

INDEX

SUPPLIERS

21st Century Yarns
Threads
Tel. 07850 616537
Yarns21stcentury@aol.com

Art Van Go
Mixed media
Tel. 01438814946
art@artvango.co.uk

Colourcraft
Mixed media, CMC, thin papers, Brusho,
Soft Form Relief paste, Soft Flow Clear
Medium, newspaper string, Shosenshi viscose
Tel. 01142421431
www.colourcraft-ltd.com

Colouricious
Wooden stamps
Tel. 01494721471
www.colouricious.com

Gillsew
Forming felt
Tel. 01494881886
admin@gillsew.co.uk

Jonathan Korejko
Handmade papers
Tel. 0800 0232478
www.timberland.co.uk

Lavinia Stamps
Stamps, stencils
Tel. 01824 710691
www.laviniastamps.com

Oliver Twists
Cocoon strippings, threads, silk fibres, kozo bark
Tel. 0191 4166016
olivertwistsretail@fsmail.net

Pfaff Sewing Machines
tom.starkey@europe.svpworldwide.com

Texere Yarns
Cocoon strippings, threads, silk fibres
Tel 01274 722191
info@texere.co.uk

The African Fabric Shop
African bark cloth
Tel. 01484 850188
www.africanfabric.co.uk

George Weil
Plasterer's cotton scrim
Tel. 01483 565800
www.georgeweil.com

USA
Dick Blick Art Materials
art supplies, Brusho paints
PO BOX 1267
Galesburg IL61402.1267
www.dickblick.com

Habu Textiles
Cricula silk pods and silk, shosenshi viscose
habu@habutextiles.com

AUSTRALIA
Beautiful Silks
Newspaper string, silk sacks
Tel. 0394 197745
info@beautifulsilks.com

Dairing
Cricula silk pods, shosenshi viscose
Tel. 61 39421 6396
info@dairing.com.au

Jellybeads of Mogo
Beads
Tel. 61 24474 2675
www.jellybeads.com.au

Open Drawer
Cricula silk pods
Tel 9889 7227
info@opendrawer.com.au

The Thread Studio
Stamps, mixed media
Tel 0892271561
www.thethreadstudio.com